Has a COW Saved Your Life?

Deborah Underwood

www.raintreepublishers.co.uk
Visit our website to find out more information about **Raintree** books.

To order:
☎ Phone 44 (0) 1865 888112
📄 Send a fax to 44 (0) 1865 314091
💻 Visit the Raintree bookshop at **www.raintreepublishers.co.uk** to browse our catalogue and order online.

First published in Great Britain by Raintree, Halley Court, Jordan Hill, Oxford OX2 8EJ, part of Harcourt Education.
Raintree is a registered trademark of Harcourt Education Ltd.

Editorial: Louise Galpine and Harriet Milles
Design: Michelle Lisseter and Bigtop
Illustrations: Paul McCaffrey (c/o Sylvie Poggio) and John Haslam
Picture Research: Mica Brancic and Maria Joannou
Production: Camilla Crask

Originated by Modern Age
Printed and bound in China by WKT Company Limited

10-digit ISBN 1 406 20471 4 (hardback)
13-digit ISBN 978 1 4062 0471 1
11 10 09 08 07
10 9 8 7 6 5 4 3 2 1

10-digit ISBN 1 406 20496 X (paperback)
13-digit ISBN 978 1 4062 0496 4
11 10 09 08 07
10 9 8 7 6 5 4 3 2 1

British Library
Cataloguing in Publication Data
Underwood, Deborah
Has a cow saved your life? - (Fusion): Medical microbiology
614.4'7
A full catalogue record for this book is available from the British Library.

Acknowledgements
The author and publisher are grateful to the following for permission to reproduce copyright material: Bridgeman Art Library/Wolverhampton Art Gallery, West Midlands, UK **p. 11**; Corbis **p. 25**; Corbis/Bettmann **p. 17**; Egypt Picture Library **p. 6**; Getty Images/Visuals Unlimited **p. 7**; Public Health Image Library **p. 5**; Science & Society Picture Library **p. 23**; Science Photo Library **pp. 27** (Biophoto Associates), **29** (CDC); Wellcome Picture Library **pp. 9, 15, 19, 20**; World Health Organisation **p. 26**.

Cover photograph of cows reproduced with permission of Masterfile/Frank Krahmer.

Illustrations by Paul McCaffrey (c/o Sylvie Poggio) and John Haslam.

The publishers would like to thank Nancy Harris and Harold Pratt for their assistance in the preparation of this book.

Every effort has been made to contact copyright holders of any material reproduced in this book. Any omissions will be rectified in subsequent printings if notice is given to the publishers.

Contents

Some words are printed in bold, **like this**. You can find out what they mean on page 30. You can also look in the box at the bottom of the page where they first appear.

Smallpox: big trouble

Imagine you are in London. The year is 1796. Your life is about to change forever.

One day, someone near you coughs. Two weeks later, you get a **fever**. Your head hurts like mad. You throw up. You start to get red spots on your body. Soon, they cover your arms and hands.

Then, spots spread to the rest of your body. They swell up into pea-sized lumps. The lumps are called **pustules**. You hurt all over. Your skin smells like rotten meat. Now you know you have **smallpox**. Smallpox is one of the world's worst diseases.

If you are lucky, you will live. If you are not lucky, you might go blind. Or you might even die. In 1796 smallpox killed thousands of people in London.

*This photo of a smallpox victim was ▶ taken 30 years ago. Smallpox pustules are filled with liquid. The liquid is full of **germs**. A germ is a tiny living creature that can cause disease.*

fever	body temperature that is higher than normal
germ	tiny living creature that can cause disease
pustule	lump on the skin filled with germs in a fluid
smallpox	disease that was often deadly

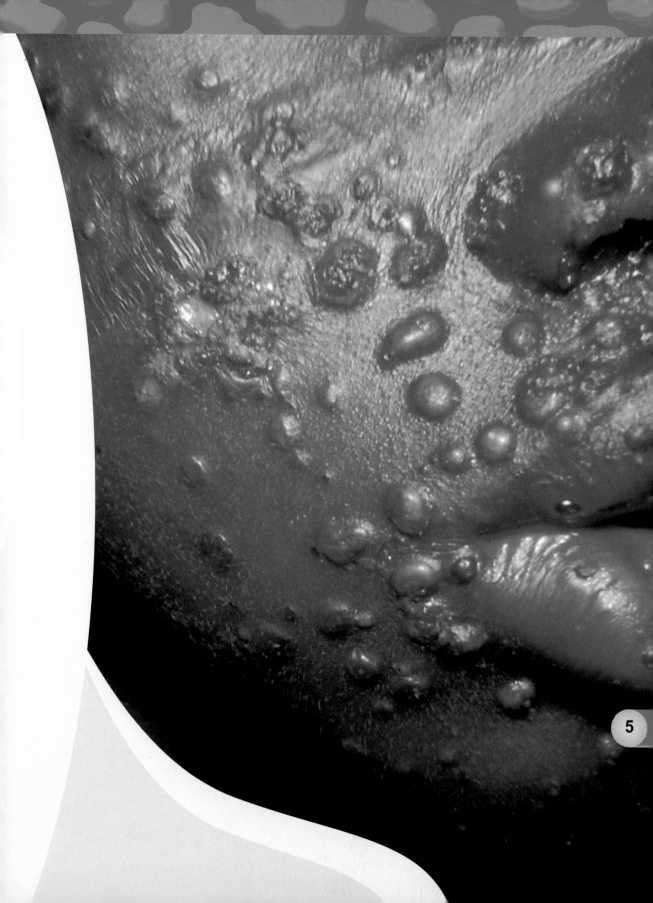

The speckled monster

People lived in fear of **smallpox** for thousands of years. Some called it "the speckled monster". People with smallpox got painful spots all over their bodies. There was no cure. Many people died.

King killer

Ramses V ruled Egypt in 1150 BC. It is likely he died of smallpox. Can you see the spots on his mummy?

microscope   something that helps you see very tiny things

Smallpox was caused by a **virus**. A virus is a tiny **germ**. The smallpox virus spread quickly. A single cough could carry millions of smallpox germs.

Smallpox swept around the world. It killed millions of people. It seemed smallpox would haunt the world forever.

Today, no one on Earth has smallpox. In 1796 a man named Edward Jenner found a way to stop it. He changed the world. He did this with the help of a cow!

Looking for answers

In 1770 Edward Jenner was a young man. He lived in a country town. Jenner wanted to help sick people. He left his home and went to London. He studied with a famous doctor. This doctor was called John Hunter.

Hunter taught his students how to find answers to questions. He taught students the **scientific method**. The scientific method is one way that scientists solve problems. To use the scientific method, you need to do six things:

Scientific method

1. First, you **observe**. To observe means to notice things.

2. You ask a question about the things you observe.

3. You form a **hypothesis**. A hypothesis is an idea of what you think will happen.

4. You do an **experiment**. An experiment is a test to check your idea.

5. You draw a **conclusion**. A conclusion is what you learn from your experiment.

6. You share what you have learned with other people.

▼ Edward Jenner learned about experiments when he studied to be a doctor.

conclusion	what you learn from a test
experiment	test that checks if an idea is right
hypothesis	idea that is based on what you know
observe	notice things
scientific method	one way scientists solve problems

The milkmaid mystery

Jenner moved back to the country. He noticed that some cows got a sickness. It was called **cowpox**. Cows with cowpox got lumps. The lumps were called **pustules**. They were a lot like **smallpox** pustules.

Sometimes a **milkmaid** milked a cow with cowpox. Sometimes the milkmaid had a cut on her hand. **Germs** from the cow could get into the cut. Then the milkmaid would get sick with cowpox, too.

Many people who worked with cows caught cowpox. Cowpox was not nearly as scary as smallpox. Cows did not die from cowpox. Neither did people. They got well in less than a week.

Once Jenner talked to a milkmaid about smallpox. She said she could not catch smallpox because she had already had cowpox. Jenner wondered if she was right.

cowpox mild sickness that cows and people can get

Scientific method checklist

☑ 1. **Observe** things

◯ 2. Ask a question

◯ 3. Form a **hypothesis**

◯ 4. Do an **experiment**

◯ 5. Draw a **conclusion**

◯ 6. Share your results with others

▲ *Milkmaids got cowpox from milking sick cows.*

Buying the pox

People had noticed something about **smallpox**. If you caught it and lived, you did not get it again. Your body remembered how to fight off the sickness. So, many people got smallpox on purpose.

A doctor would scratch their arms with a knife. Then, he took **pus** from smallpox **pustules**. Pus is fluid full of **germs**. He put pus in the scratches on their arms. The pus made them get sick. This was called **inoculation**. People called it "buying the pox".

The doctors took the pus from people with mild smallpox. Most people who got inoculated got mild cases, too.

But some of the people did *not* get mild smallpox. They got very sick. Some even died. While they were sick, they could spread smallpox to others.

inoculation	being given a mild sickness to prevent a worse case later on
pus	germ-filled fluid

▼ Smallpox inoculation was risky. People could get very sick.

1 The doctor made a cut on a healthy person's arm.

2 He took pus from someone with mild smallpox.

4 The healthy person caught smallpox.

3 The doctor put the smallpox pus on the healthy person's scratch.

13

Finding clues

Jenner began to make **observations**. Observations are things you notice. He **observed** everything he could about **smallpox** and **cowpox**. He looked for clues. The clues might help him find a way to stop smallpox.

Jenner was a doctor. He gave **inoculations** to many farmworkers. This means he gave them the smallpox **virus**. He noticed that some people did not get sick. These people had already had cowpox.

Jenner made more observations. He found lots of people who had been sick with cowpox. They all seemed to be safe from smallpox. They did not catch it when he put smallpox **pus** on their scratches.

Jenner began to get excited. He asked this question:

Does cowpox stop people from getting smallpox?

observation   thing you notice
udders   bag-like part of a cow where milk is stored

Scientific method checklist

✓ 1. **Observe** things

✓ 2. Ask a question

○ 3. Form a **hypothesis**

○ 4. Do an **experiment**

○ 5. Draw a **conclusion**

○ 6. Share your results with others

▼ *This is a drawing of a cow's **udders**. The **pustules** are from cowpox. People sometimes got cowpox from a cow. These people seemed to be safe from smallpox.*

Jenner's idea

Jenner had **observed** (noticed) everything he could about **smallpox** and **cowpox**. He had asked a question. Next, he formed a **hypothesis**.

A hypothesis is an idea. It is an idea based on what you know. It is not a wild guess. For example, you notice that your little sister likes to play with your yo-yo. One day, your yo-yo is gone from your room. A hypothesis would be that your little sister took it. A wild guess would be that aliens sneaked into your room and stole it.

Jenner had observed many clues. These clues helped him form a hypothesis. This was Jenner's hypothesis:

I will give people cowpox on purpose. It will keep them safe from smallpox.

The idea seemed to make sense. But Jenner needed to check his idea. He needed to test his idea with an **experiment**.

Scientific method checklist

☑ 1. **Observe** things
☑ 2. Ask a question
☑ 3. Form a **hypothesis**
◯ 4. Do an **experiment**
◯ 5. Draw a **conclusion**
◯ 6. Share your results with others

If I give people cowpox, they will never get smallpox.

17

▲ *Jenner's idea was one of the greatest in history!*

The boy and the cow

Jenner thought of an **experiment**. He would use **cowpox pus** to give someone cowpox. Later, he would try to give the same person **smallpox**. If that person did not get smallpox, Jenner's idea might be right.

But Jenner could not just go and buy cowpox **virus**. He had to wait for a cow or person to catch cowpox. He waited many years. Finally, in 1796 a person caught cowpox.

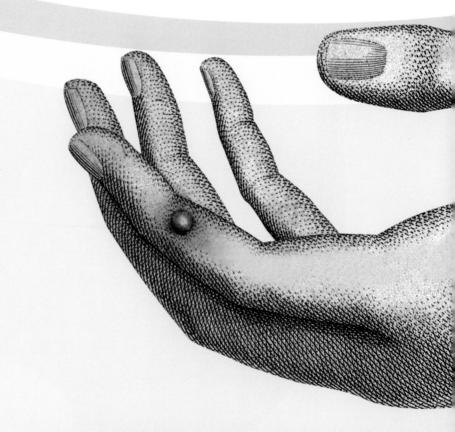

A **milkmaid** called Sarah Nelmes went to see Jenner. She had a cowpox **pustule** on her hand.

Sarah had poked her finger on a thorn. Then, she had milked a cow called Blossom. Blossom had cowpox. Sarah got cowpox through her wound.

Now Jenner could do his experiment!

▼ Jenner drew this picture of Sarah Nelmes' hand in 1798. The lumps you can see are the cowpox pustules.

▼ Jenner did his experiment on an eight-year-old boy called James Phipps.

Watching and waiting

Jenner picked a young boy called James Phipps to help with his **experiment**. Jenner made two small cuts in the boy's arm. Then, he took some **cowpox pus** from Sarah Nelmes. He put the pus in James's wounds. Would James get cowpox? Nine days later, James got a bit sick. But on the tenth day, he was fine again.

It was time for the next part of the experiment. Jenner found someone with **smallpox**. He took pus (**germ**-filled fluid) from one of the smallpox **pustules**. He made more cuts in James's arm. He put the smallpox pus in. He waited. Would the boy get sick?

James did not get smallpox! Jenner was very happy. Still he wanted to make sure. He tried over and over to give James smallpox. James stayed healthy.

Scientific method checklist

- ✓ 1. **Observe** things
- ✓ 2. Ask a question
- ✓ 3. Form a **hypothesis**
- ✓ 4. Do an **experiment**
- ◯ 5. Draw a **conclusion**
- ◯ 6. Share your results with others

More tests

Jenner needed to do more **experiments**. He gave **cowpox** to more people. Then, three of them were given **smallpox pus**. They did not get smallpox.

Jenner drew a **conclusion**. This means he summed up the results of his tests. His conclusion was that his **hypothesis**, or idea, was right. Giving people cowpox did protect them from smallpox.

Jenner's tests would save millions of lives. People would not need to have smallpox **germs** put in cuts in their arms. Instead, they could have cowpox germs. It was safer to give people cowpox. Cowpox did not kill people.

Jenner dreamed his work would wipe out smallpox. He was right. But it took much longer than he hoped.

A new name

The Latin word for cow *is* vacca. *Jenner called his way of preventing smallpox* "vaccination". *He called the cowpox pus he used* "vaccine". *Today, the word* vaccination *means putting weak germs in the body. Then the weak germs teach the body to fight off sickness.*

vaccination   using weak germs to teach the body to fight off sickness

vaccine   germ-filled fluid used to vaccinate people

Scientific method checklist

- ✓ 1. **Observe** things
- ✓ 2. Ask a question
- ✓ 3. Form a **hypothesis**
- ✓ 4. Do an **experiment**
- ◯ 5. Draw a **conclusion**
- ◯ 6. Share your results with others

▼ *Jenner used these tools during vaccinations. He used them to make scratches on people's arms.*

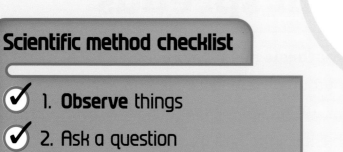

Jenner's plan spreads

Many people must test a **hypothesis** (idea) before it is accepted. Jenner wrote to a group of scientists. He told them about his test on James. He hoped they would write about it. Instead the scientists thought his idea was too strange.

So Jenner wrote his own book. He printed a lot of copies. Other doctors read the book. They tested Jenner's idea. It worked for them, too. Many thought Jenner was a hero.

Not everyone liked the idea of using **cowpox vaccine** to prevent **smallpox**. Some people thought it was wrong. Others feared that giving people cowpox would turn them into cows!

In time, more people accepted Jenner's hypothesis. Yet it would be nearly 200 years before smallpox was gone for good.

Forbidden

After Jenner's discovery, some doctors kept giving people weak cases of smallpox. Then, sick people would sometimes spread smallpox to others. Giving people smallpox on purpose was finally forbidden in the mid-1800s.

✓ 1. **Observe** things

✓ 2. Ask a question

✓ 3. Form a **hypothesis**

✓ 4. Do an **experiment**

✓ 5. Draw a **conclusion**

✓ 6. Share your results with others

▼ *James Gillray's cartoon from 1802 shows what people feared about the cowpox vaccine. The people in the picture are turning into cows!*

The speckled monster dies

Smallpox was wiped out of one country after another. In 1980 a world health group said smallpox was finally gone for good. The speckled monster was dead!

Most people do not get smallpox **vaccinations** anymore. But some scientists do. So do some doctors and nurses. They get it just in case smallpox ever comes back.

Because of Edward Jenner, people no longer live in fear of smallpox. By using the **scientific method**, he solved one of the world's worst problems. He could not have done it without James Phipps. He could not have done it without Blossom the cow. So, the next time you see a cow, say thank you!

This magazine from ▶ 1980 told the world that smallpox had been wiped out.

WORLD HEALTH
THE MAGAZINE OF THE WORLD HEALTH ORGANIZATION · MAY 1980

smallpox is dead!

This person is being ▼ vaccinated against smallpox. The last case of smallpox was in 1978.

The scientific method

Here is how Jenner found a way to stop **smallpox**:

Scientific method checklist

✓	1. Observe things	Jenner noticed that people who had already had cowpox didn't get smallpox.
✓	2. Ask a question	Jenner asked this question: does cowpox keep people from getting smallpox?
✓	3. Form a hypothesis	Jenner had the idea that if he gave people cowpox on purpose, it would keep them safe from smallpox.
✓	4. Do an experiment	Jenner gave James Phipps cowpox. Then, he tried to give him smallpox.
✓	5. Draw a conclusion	James did not catch smallpox. Jenner believed that his idea was right.
✓	6. Share your results with others	Jenner wrote his results in a book so others could try his test, too.

7. THANK COW!

Locked away

Today, smallpox **germs** are in only two laboratories. One is in the United States. The other is in Russia. The germs are locked away in freezers.

Why are the germs kept? Some people think we will learn things by studying them. But others believe the smallpox germs should be destroyed.

100 DOSES ℞ only
Smallpox Vaccine
Dried, Calf Lymph Type
Dryvax®
Dose: Approx. 2.5 µL Reconsti

This tiny bottle ▶ contains smallpox **vaccine**. The vaccine has saved millions of lives.

Glossary

conclusion what you learn from a test. Jenner wrote his conclusion in a book so others could read it.

cowpox mild sickness that cows and people can get. Many of Jenner's patients got cowpox.

experiment test that checks if an idea is right. Jenner did an experiment to see if cowpox prevented smallpox.

fever body temperature that is higher than normal

germ tiny living creature that can cause disease

hypothesis idea that is based on what you know. After he asked a question, Jenner formed a hypothesis.

inoculation being given a mild sickness to prevent a worse case later on. Before Jenner's tests, doctors gave people inoculations to give them mild cases of smallpox.

microscope something that helps you see very tiny things

milkmaid woman who milks cows

observation thing you notice. Jenner's observations made him think that cowpox might prevent smallpox.

observe notice things. Jenner observed that people who had already had cowpox were safe from smallpox.

pus germ-filled fluid. Jenner put cowpox pus in people's arms to give them cowpox.

pustule lump on the skin filled with germs in a fluid. Smallpox and cowpox both gave people pustules.

scientific method one way scientists solve problems. Jenner used the scientific method to find a better way to prevent smallpox.

smallpox disease that was often deadly. Smallpox killed millions of people.

udders bag-like part of a cow where milk is stored

vaccination using weak germs to teach the body to fight off sickness. Today, there are vaccinations for many sicknesses.

vaccine germ-filled fluid used to vaccinate people

virus tiny germ that can make people sick. Smallpox is caused by a virus.

Want to know more?

Books to read

- *A Painful History of Medicine: Pox, Pus and Plague (Freestyle Express)*, John Townsend (Raintree, 2002)
- *Horrible Science: Deadly Diseases,* Nick Arnold (Scholastic Hippo, 2000)
- *The Smallpox Slayer,* Alan Brown (Hodder Headline, 2001)

Websites

- http://science.howstuffworks.com/virus-human.htm
  Find out more about how viruses work.
- http://www.kidshealth.org/kid/health_problems/infection/smallpox.html
  Find out more about smallpox and the smallpox vaccine.

Find out more about the world's most scary diseases in ***World's Worst Germs***.

Your body has its own special army to fight disease. Find out how it works in ***Body Warriors***.

Index